HISTORY

OF

DELAWARE COUNTY

FOR THE

PAST CENTURY.

By Hon. John M. Broomall.

Read before the Delaware County Institute of Science and Filed with the Congressional Librarian at Washington.

Media, Pa:
Vernon & Cooper, Steam Power Book Printers,
1876.

History of Delaware County.

To the Delaware County Institue of Science:—

The undersigned, appointed at the meeting of the Institute in May last to prepare a brief history of Delaware County for the century just now closing, respectfully submits the following report:

The appointment was made pursuant to a recommendation of the National and State authorities that such outlines of history be prepared for every City and County in the Union, to be read on the Fourth of July, 1876, and preserved as matter of local history for future reference and use. What is desired is to make a record of the progress of the County materially, morally, and politically during the last century.—The task imposed is rendered easy up to 1860 by the elaborate and valuable "History of Delaware County," published in that year by the President of the Institute, Dr. George Smith. Indeed, little has been attempted prior to that date except to extract from that work in a condensed form such materials as were supposed to be appropriate to a brief review of the century called for. Tendering thanks to the author for the valuable aid rendered by the work is but feebly expressing the obligations of the people of the County to their historian.

The territory embraced within the limits of Delaware County contained the earliest European settlements in Pennsylvania, but the County as a municipal organization was not created until 1789. The first settlers were Swedes who came about the year 1640, and located themselves along the Delaware River. Many of the present inhabitants of the County are descendants of these people and their names, sometimes more or less changed, are still common among us. The settlements were within the limits of Chester County, one of the three laid off by Penn at the founding of his colony, the other two being Philadelphia and Bucks. These Counties abutted on the eastward upon the Delaware, and extended westward without definite limits. In 1729 the

County of Lancaster was created on the west of Chester, and thus the boundaries of Chester County became fixed. They remained the same until the division of the County in 1789.

Delaware County owes its existence to a contest about the seat of Justice of Chester County. The little village of Chester, being on the river, and about the middle of the settlements, was the seat of government of the colony from its commencement until the laying out of Philadelphia.—After that time it continued to be the seat ot Justice of Chester County. As the settlements extended westward the location of the Courts and records became more and more inconvenient to the average population, and from this arose the project of removing the seat of Justice inland. The site selected was a place in Goshen Township, called "The Turk's Head" from the sign of the tavern which constituted almost the entire village. The movement began in 1780 and lasted some half dozen years, ending in success. The new seat of Justice was called West Chester, and the first Court was held there in November, 1786.

The people of Chester and its vicinity were so exasperated by what had been done, that they applied to the Legislature and in 1789 procured an act erecting Delaware County out of the eastern portion of the old County and fixing the County seat at Chester. The townships so cut off were Aston, Bethel, Chester, Concord, Darby, Upper Darby, Upper Chichester, Lower Chichester, Edgmont, Haverford, Marple, Middletown, Nether Providence, Upper Providence, Newtown, Radnor, Ridley, Springfield, Tinicum and parts of Birmingham and Thornbury. The boundaries of these townships remain nearly the same, no new ones having been created, and only that ot Aston and Concord changed.

The extreme length of the County is twenty miles and the extreme breadth fourteen, and it contains about one hundred and sixty-five square miles. At the first census in 1790 the population was 9483. The increase to 1800 was 3326; that to 1810, 1925; to 1820, 84; to 1830, 2513; to 1840, 2468; to 1850, 4888; to 1860, 5918; and to 1870, 8906, making the population in 1870, 39,403. The last rate of increase continued would make the present number of inhabitants over forty-six thousand. The small increase given by the census returns between 1810 and 1820, only 84, may be an error, due to careless enumerating previously, or if correct, it may have arisen from the troubles with England deterring emigration.

Chester is the oldest town in the State. The first settlers called the place Upland, a name which it bore until Penn gave it the present one in 1682. The date of its first settlement is unknown, but in 1668 it had become the chief town of the Upper Delaware settlements, and the place where the Courts were held. In 1682, Penn took formal possession of his new colony of Pennsylvania and established his government at Chester, where it remained a year or two, when the newer City of Philadelphia robbed it of its honor.

It has been said that the reason Penn did not locate his City at Chester was the fear that it might not be within his boundaries, and in fact according to the letter of his charter from the crown it is not. But the beautiful highland lying between the two rivers was doubtless sufficient to induce the change; and to the small vessels of that day and with the channel of the Delaware as it was then, Philadelphia was about as accessible to the Ocean as Chester.

In 1776 the population of Chester was probably about four hundred. Dr. Smith, in his history, page 286, gives us one hundred and sixty-eight as the number of taxables in Chester township in 1775. The Borough being in the township, probably contained the half of these—eighty-four; assuming five persons to one taxable and we have four hundred and twenty as the probable population one hundred years ago.

It is very doubtful whether the number of inhabitants increased at all between 1776 and 1827. At the latter date the whole number of buildings in the Town was but seventy, including barns, stables, and shops; and six persons to a building is a full estimate. Between 1830 and 1840 the Philadelphia, Wilmington and Baltimore Railroad was built, passing through Chester, and extensive stone quarries were opened in the vicinity furnishing large quantities of stone to the Delaware Breakwater. These enterprises gave an impetus to the town which in 1840 increased its number of buildings to two hundred and twenty-four and its population to something over seven hundred.

In 1850 quite a change had taken place. The seat of Justice had been removed, manufacturers had discovered the convenience of the town to the sources of the materials they needed as well as to the market for their products, and even the old residents had begun to think that the Delaware might furnish some material good besides fish.

The census returns of 1850 gave the number of inhabitants as 1667, and those of 1860 as 4631. In 1866 the Borough became a City by act of Legislature, and in 1870 the number of inhabitants was 9485. A similar increase since 1870 would make the present population over 15,000. The wealth and all the material interests of the town have increased in like proportion. Manufactories of cotton, wool and iron have sprung up all over the place, and probably no town of its size in the State exceeds it in industry and enterprise.

The history of Chester during the century is a remarkable one. After a state of almost absolute inertness for sixty-five years of that period an increase of population from seven hundred to fifteen thousand in the remaining thirty-five years, may well suggest an inquiry into the causes, and some of these are not difficult to see. Something has been attributed to the removal of the seat of Justice, and no doubt that had its effect. A certain proportion of the people of a county town depends upon the administering of Justice; the attorneys and other officers of the Courts, the Justices of the Peace, constables, tipstaves, tavern keepers, waiters, hostlers and a variety of similar non-producers, who hang about the public offices with the hope of picking up an occasional fee or gratuity.

Added to these and aiding them in their sphere of usefulness are the large and small politicians of the County, who always gravitate to the County seat unless they can make more by remaining away and holding it up to public obloquy. Where these elements constitute substantially the entire population it will be readily seen that the general result is stagnation. Progress may be a thing talked of in jolly moments around a tavern bar, but it will be as we talk of the antipodes, the prehistoric or the coming man, something afar off in either time or space or both.

If the place should once outgrow these elements, forcing them into a subordinate position, where they belong, as Philadelphia has done, the Courts and their surroundings will become relatively less injurious; but Chester in 1850, had not outgrown them, though there were indications that it might do so, and the removal of the seat of Justice, doubtless, acted as one cause of the great awakening.

Another, and a greater cause, was the discovery of the local advantages of Chester for factories. Philadelphia was becoming a great manufacturing city, and it was natural that the high rents and expensive living of that city should direct the attention of producers to the neighboring towns. Chester is upon tide water, about as convenient to coal, iron and other materials, as Philadelphia, and much more accessible to the outside world, being at the head of winter navigation in severe seasons, and being the point to which vessels bound upwards usually come without towing. The water power of the county had been already appropriated and in many places steam had come to be used to compensate for the irregularity of the water power. By this means an opportunity was afforded of comparing the two powers, and it was ascertained that steam upon the tide is quite equal, if not superior in point of economy to water power inland. In fact for some years, factory sites on streams remote from the river have been abandoned for steam on the tide.

The result of all this is, that an entire new population has taken posession of the City of Chester, establishing places of productive industry everywhere, building up its vacant lots and extending the town beyond its incorporated limits on all sides except where the Delaware interposes to prevent it. Many of these incomers are from the county, seeking faster modes of becoming rich than cultivating the soil, or if not changing their business, at least seeking a larger and better field for it. Many come from other states, and very many from foreign countries.

As it is the energetic who emigrate, these people brought with them more than the average energy of the places from which they came, and their advent into Chester was very much like that of the European settlers among the aborigines. After a little natural jealousy had subsided, the natives, unable to resist the stream of progress, have fallen into the current to aid and be aided by it, or have retired to vegetate upon the profits arising from the sale of their lands rendered valuable without their aid and apparently against their will. The Chester of half a century ago forms but an insignificant constituent of the Chester of 1876.

Next to Chester, Marcus Hook appears to be the oldest town in Pennsylvania. It was erected into a market town by Penn in 1701, by letters patent under the name of Chichester, and empowered to hold a weekly market and fair. The letters patent speak of it as "aforetime commonly called Marcus Hook, and of late usually called Chichester." But the new name did not supplant the old one. The Legislature in the present charter enacted in 1833, adopted the "aforetime" title. Indeed the place had never been called by any other name except in a few public documents at least a century old.

Marcus Hook is quite equal to Chester as an eligible site

for manufactories, if not superior. The river channel is nearer the shore, as well as deeper and broader, and the place has not been shut off from the ocean by ice at any time for half a century. Probably the accident of a few enterprising men locating themselves at Chester between 1840 and 1850 fixed that as the city instead of Marcus Hook. Before 1830 the two places were rivals in inertness and obscurity, surprised occasionally by the erection of a new dwelling on the ruins of one rotted down. Within a few years Marcus Hook has made some spasmodic efforts to imitate her more fortunate sister, and unless the old inhabitants succeed in preventing the influx of energy from abroad, a dozen years more will probably develop the natural advantages of the place and make it again the rival of Chester.

In 1850 the population of Marcus Hook was 492. Since then the census returns incorporate it with the township of Lower Chichester, in which it lies, leaving us to conjecture the number of inhabitants. Probably six hundred in 1870 and seven hundred and fifty now would be a close estimate.

Darby was one of the primitive settlements. The early travel among the colonists was mainly up and down the river, and of necessity it crossed the streams at first at the head of tide water. The places of crossing were favorable sites for settlements unless the river shore opposite afforded peculiar commercial advantages as at Marcus Hook and Chester. This determined the location of Darby at the head of tide on Darby creek, the country between that and the river being low, formerly chiefly covered with water at high tide, and kept habitable now by artificial banks.

Dr. Smith tells us that before the close of 1683 Penn's followers "had gained a very permanent footing at Chester, Marcus Hook, Darby and Haverford." But up to 1860 the population of Darby had only reached seven hundred and eighty. Since then however, manufacturing enterprises have started there and in 1870 the inhabitants numbered twelve hundred and five. Probably now they would reach fifteen hundred.

The Borough of Darby was erected in 1853 out of the town and part of the township of Darby.

The Borough of Media, the present seat of Justice of the county, was chartered in 1850. It is located very nearly in the middle of the county, on the high land between Ridley and Crum creeks, about five miles from the river and is from two to four hundred feet above the ocean level. The eastern portion of the town is comparatively level, but the western, sloping towards Ridley creek, is quite hilly, making it difficult to locate streets and roads in that direction. The vicinity presents mountain scenery on a small scale, and is very much admired. The high and healthy location, the pure air and the wild roads along the wooded streams, suggestive of pleasure driving, fill the town with summer visitors, from the neighboring city, from which it is distant only thirteen miles.

Like the county, the county town owes its existence to a contest about the seat of Justice. For many years the popularity of Chester had been upon the wane. Its people had given offence by endeavoring to rule the county, and only partially succeeding. Jurors, parties and witnesses believed themselves to be imposed upon by high charges, and they knew themselves to be sneered at and ridiculed by the tavern idlers who constituted most of the *elite* of the town. Besides this, the water was bad and the place was charged with being unhealthy, especially to people from the higher lands, a charge with little or no foundation, for Chester has its full proportion of old men and women in a population congregated from a wide range of climate.

In 1820 an ineffectual attempt was made to remove the seat of Justice to a more central point. In 1845 the effort was renewed, and in 1847 an act Assembly was passed submitting the question to the votes of the people at the next succeeding election. Not knowing or not properly considering how migratory a seat of Justice would become if its location were voted upon at every election, the people of Chester consented to this act. The result was just what might have been anticipated, a majority of seven hundred and fifty-two in a vote of about three thousand. The location not having been since changed, it is hardly necessary to say that the experiment of submitting it to the votes of the people has never been tried in Delaware county since.

In the census returns of 1870 the population of Media is given as 1045. It is probably now about 1400. At the time of the removal, a store, a tavern and two or three farm houses constituted the entire town.

By a provision in the Charter the sale of intoxicating drinks is forever prohibited within the Borough limits. The consequence is that Media is one of the most peaceable and orderly places in the country.

There are five schools supported by the public and three by private subscriptions. The latter are a large and well patronized school for girls and young women, a large boarding school for boys and a select school for both sexes. All these, public and private, are in a flourishing condition.

The Court House is a large and substantial structure, built of stone and brick, the first story being fireproof. It is eighty-two feet by fifty, with two wings, each thirty-eight feet square. The Court room, about sixty feet by forty-six, is in the second story. It is approached by two iron stairways in front and a wooden one in the rear, all leading from the interior of the first story. This story contains the offices of the Prothonotary and Clerk of the Criminal Court, the Register and Clerk of the Orphans' Court, the Recorder of Deeds, the Sheriff, the County Treasurer, the Commissioners and Superintendent of Common Schools. The building is erected in the middle of a rectangle 500 feet by 240, surrounded by streets. It is enclosed by an iron fence and is beautifully ornamented with shade and forest trees, many of them of rare varieties. The Court House square contains no other buildings. The prison is situated across the street from it, and is a substantial building adapted to the Pennsylvania system of solitary confinement, a system of very doubtful expediency.

Media is plentifully supplied with places of religious worship. One Episcopal, one Methodist, one African Methodist, one Presbyterian, one Roman Catholic, one Baptist and two Friends' Meeting Houses. Besides these buildings there are others of a *quasi* public character the buildings owned and occupied by the First National Bank of Media, the Delaware County Institute of Science, the Delaware County Mutual Insurance Company and the Charter House Association—all substantial structures adapted to use rather than ornament.

The Borough owns a dam and water power on Ridley creek from which water is forced into a basin located on the highest point within the chartered limits, sufficient for any imaginable increase of population for another century; and the Media Gas Company lights the town with coal gas at a moderate cost.

South Chester and North Chester Boroughs are mere extensions of the City of Chester beyond the incorporated limits, the former on the southwest and the latter on the north. The same paved streets and brick sidewalks continue with nothing to designate the line where one jurisdiction ends and the other begins. South Chester was incorporated in 1866, and in 1870 the number of inhabitants was 1242, the number of voters in 1875 was 299, and judging from this the present population exceeds 1500. North Chester was incorporated in 1873. The voters in 1875 numbered 199, so that the present population exceeds 1000.

The Borough of Upland adjoins Chester City and North Chester Borough. It was founded by the late John P. Crozer about the year 1845 and the entire Borough is still owned mainly by his children. It was incorporated in 1869 and in 1870 the population was 1341. It is probably now 1600. Extensive Cotton Mills make up the great business of the place, and the neat rows of comfortable brick houses, the Church, Sunday School and Library testify to the regard the enterprising owners have for the population in their employment.

The City of Chester and the surrounding Boroughs of North and South Chester and Upland as well as parts of the adjoining townships of Chester, Lower Chichester and Ridley constitute really but a single large manufacturing town with a population of more than twenty thousand, rapidly approaching Marcus Hook to absorb it, and destined in a very few years to connect with Philadelphia along the highlands occupied by the new route of the Philadelphia, Wilmington and Baltimore Railroad, and the old King's Highway. The river shore between Chester and Marcus Hook, must become the port of Philadelphia, unless that city is content to give up its foreign commerce altogether; and it is not unsafe to predict that the child is living who will see the southern limits of what will be substantially the City of Philadelphia at the Delaware State line.

It is impossible within the limits allowed to enumerate the factories, mills, machine shops, and other business establishments of Chester and its surroundings, or to name the enterprising men who have made the place what it is; and to designate a few of either out of the many would be an invidious task.

Besides these municipalities there are many towns mainly devoted to manufactures not yet arisen to the dignity of corporations. Those containing one hundred inhabitants and over are Village Green, Rockdale and Crozerville in Aston township; Chelsea in Bethel township; Concordville in Concord; Leiperville, Ridley Park, Eddystone and Norwood in Ridley; Sharon Hill in Darby: Howellville in Edgmont; Coopertown in Haverford; Lima, Lenni, Glen Riddle and Knowlton in Middletown; Newtown Square in Newtown; Waterville and South Media in Nether Providence; Morton in Springfield; Morgan's corner in Radnor; Glen Mills in Thornbury; Linwood in Lower Chichester; and Clifton, Garrettford, Kellyville and Fernwood in Upper Darby.

All these towns including the City of Chester, are mainly the work of the last thirty-five years, and during the same period the rate of increase in the county, has been such as, if continued, will give us a quarter of a million inhabitants before the lapse of another century.

One hundred years ago the great business of the county was agriculture, and all other kinds of business were subservient to it; the land was devoted almost entirely to the raising of grain and the raising and fattening of cattle. The growth of Philadelphia and the filling up of the country around it have changed all this. Agriculture is still a leading interest, but its products are different now. Instead of sending out of the county for sale wheat, corn and beef, we send milk, butter, hay, garden vegetables and small fruits, articles formerly supplied to Philadelphia from a nearer source. For half a century, the corn, wheat and oats raised in the county have not been sufficient for its own use.

Besides this change, the cultivation of the soil has become second in importance to manufactures and mechanical productions. For some years the great productive business of the county has been the manufacturing of woolen goods and of iron, the last embracing the making of edge tools, steam engines and other machinery.

Chester, Ridley, Crum and Darby creeks with several smaller streams cross the county emptying into the Delaware. The fall on each of these streams is from one to two hundred feet, affording many water powers of moderate size. In 1827 the number of these occupied was 158, and the number unoccupied 42. Of those occupied 38 were used for flour mills, 53 for saw mills, 27 for cotton and woolen mills, 11 for paper mills and 5 for manufactures of iron.

In 1850 a great change had taken place in these mill seats; the saw mills had mainly disappeared with the surplus timber of the county; the lumber for building and even for fencing had come to be mainly supplied from the banks of the Susquehanna and elsewhere. The increase of population in the county, and its contiguity to Philadelphia had turned the farms over to the dairy and horticulture and the flour mills mainly vanished with the wheat and corn fields leaving place to manufactures of cotton and wool. In 1827 the products of these were made by hand looms except in a single instance.

Lewis & Phillips in 1825 established the first power loom mill in the county. John P. Crozer began weaving with power looms in 1830 and others soon followed, until in 1850 most of the water powers of the county were used for these products. All over the county manufacturing villages had sprung up, giving the farmer a market almost at his own door for his milk, butter, eggs, poultry, and the products of his garden, paying him largely for the lack of a wheat crop even if, as was often the case, he had to buy his own flour.

After 1850 another change took place ; the water powers began to be deserted by these establishments for locations on the tide, coal had begun to supplant water power, both by reason of convenience and economy, and the factories sought the places handiest to that new force. This has built up Chester and its suburbs, and while manufactures have steadily increased since that time, it is no uncommon thing now to see the ruins of old abandoned factories crumbling into the unused streams that formerly kept their busy wheels and busy hands moving.

In 1827 the number of persons employed in the manufacture of cotton and woolen goods in the county was 643, in 1870 the number had increased to 4030, and the value of the products during the same period rose from $400,000 per annum to nearly $7,000,000. Since 1870 the business has been steadily on the increase, except that the present stagnation in all industries is affecting that also. The number of looms now running in the county is about 5000, and the number of spindles 200,000.

Paper making was first commenced in the county at Ivy Mills in Concord township, by Thomas Wilcox in 1720 His descendants of the same family name still own and use the same mill site for the same purpose. A branch of the establishment was afterwards fixed in Glen Mills in Thornbury township, by the same parties, and at this latter place the paper used by the Government for the currency is made.

In 1860 there were 119 hands employed in making $180,898 worth of materials into $345,000 worth of paper, and in 1870 the workmen had increased to 135, the materials to $260,080 in value, and the products to $383,000. There is no reason to suppose that the same rate of increase has not continued up to the present time.

The first railroad in the United States was built in Nether Providence township, in this county, by Thomas Leiper, in 1806. The engineer was John Thompson, the father of the late President of the Pennsylvania Railroad Company, and the original draft of the road is in the museum of the Delaware County Institute. The length of the road was a mile and a quarter, and it was constructed and used for years in carrying stone from the quarries on Crum Creek to the landing.

The Columbia, Lancaster and Philadelphia Railroad Company was chartered in 1826. The road ran through the townships of Radnor and Haverford. The Pennsylvania Railroad Company, the present possessor of the road, was chartered in 1846; the route is now changed so as to run through the township of Radnor only. When the Columbia Railroad was projected, there was considerable alarm in this county, lest interior competition would so lower prices in the Philadelphia markets as to break up the farmers; here and when steam was introduced as a motive power, horses would certainly become valueless; yet grain and horses have steadily risen in price ever since.

The Philadelphia, Wilmington & Baltimore Railroad Company was chartered in 1836, and in 1838 the road was in operation. In 1872 the company constructed what is known as the Darby Improvement branch, by which the route from Chester to Philadelphia was changed from the marsh lands along the river to the higher table land westward. The old road between those two cities has been since sold or leased for a long term of years to the Reading Railroad Company by which it is now operated.

This latter company has within a few years become the owner of a tract of land of about three hundred and fifty acres on the river above and adjoining Marcus Hook, and being the owner of the Front street railroad which connects the old route of the Baltimore railroad with that land, it has become one of the railroads of the county.

The West Chester & Philadelphia Railroad Company was chartered in 1848. The road enters the county from the west in the valley of Chester creek, and continues in the valley to Glen Riddle, from which place it crosses the country through Media to Philadelphia.

The Chester Creek Railroad Company was chartered in 1866. This road connects the West Chester railroad with Chester by running from Lenni down the valley of Chester Creek. It also connects with the Baltimore Direct Railroad at Pennellton, the owners of which were chartered in 1853. Intersected as the county is in various directions by these means of communication, it is safe to say that there is no point within its borders five miles distant from a railroad.

Our county has its full share of business corporations. Among them are the Delaware County National Bank chartered in 1814 by the State, and converted into a National Bank in 1864, the First National Bank of Chester and the First National Bank of Media, both chartered in 1864. The last is located at Media and the other two at Chester.

The Delaware County Mutual Insurance Company, at Media, and the Chester Mutual Insurance Company, at Chester, insure against losses by fire, but the most of this insuring is done by companies elsewhere. The local companies being preferred partly on account of the cheapness of their rates, and partly because their managers are well known, obtain all the risks they will take; but this is only a small portion of the demand for insurance.

Building Associations, an invention of very modern times, have had their full share of patronage since their first introduction in 1852, and through their operations hundreds of laboring men and others of small means, who otherwise would not have saved a dollar, are now living in their own comfortable homes. In the hands of conscientious men, these institutions are a great blessing to people of small resources, but they are liable to abuse by harsh, hard and unscrupulous managers.

The people of our County are essentially a newspaper reading community. The various Philadelphia papers circulate largely among us and our local press is deservedly well patronized. The oldest existing paper of the County is *The Delaware County Republican.* It was established in 1833 and still continues with the same name, the same owner and the same general character. Its politics were Whig while that party lasted, and afterwards Republican. Its columns have always been devoted to the cause of liberty, temperance and good morals. In 1855 *The Delaware County American* commenced. It is still published in the same ownership, and its general character and standing, as well as its political course and the principles inculcated, have always been similar to and of like high moral tone with those of the *Republican.* In 1835 the first number of the *Delaware County Democrat* appeared. At the end of the year it was suspended and after a long trance it revived in 1867 and is still published. Its politics have been generally Democratic. In 1873 *The Democratic Pilot* and *The Weekly Mail* were first issued, the former

Democratic and the latter neutral in politics. The *Daily News* the only daily paper published in the County was established the same year. *The Delaware County Advocate* commenced in 1869. It is independent in politics, but of Republican proclivities, and devoted to the cause of temperance.

Several papers which were of importance in their day have ceased to exist. The first ever published in the County was a neutral paper called the *Post Boy*. It appeared in 1819 and in 1820 it changed owners, name and politics, becoming the *Upland Union*, and democratic. Under this name it continued until 1842. In 1856 it was revived for a life of six months. The *Weekly Visitor* was published from 1826 to 1833. Its chief political feature was its opposition to the order of Free Masons.

In 1848 Dr. Joshua W. Ash, a member of this body, published the first map of Delaware County. The material for it was obtained with great care and much labor, partly from the records of the county and private title papers and partly from actual surveys. It exhibits not only the towns, roads and streams, the school houses, places of religious worship, post offices and mills, but the farm boundary lines, with the names of the owners; and for a work of so much detail it is singularly accurate. It is believed to be the first instance in America in which so large a district of country has been mapped so minutely as to show the comparative size, shape and ownership of all the homesteads of even a few acres. Within half a dozen years other maps of the county have been published, largely copied from this one and showing the recent changes.

In the moral aspect of the subject, the religious denominations of the county demand the first attention. Constituting as they did almost the entire colony of Penn, the Friends for the first half century greatly outnumbered all the other sects. The colony, however, being by the benign system of its founder open equally to all, other denominations had obtained considerable footing prior to the commencement of the century now closing, and during that century the Friends have become but a small portion of the religious element of the county. The decendants of these people, however, constitute the majority of the population, and their distinctive peculiarities sensibly affect the entire county. The hostility to oppression, whether on account of sex, race or opinions, the opposition to the use of intoxicating drinks, to judicial and profane swearing, to war, and especially to "playing soldier" in time of peace, which characterize us, came from this source. Persons from elsewhere visiting our Courts, are surprised to find the oath rarely taken by either juror or witness.

It is to be remembered that hostility to war did not prevent the descendants of the Friends nor the Friends themselves from engaging in it to suppress the recent rebellion. Probably they saw the issue and while they did not hate war the less they hated slavery more. It has been truly remarked that during that struggle the Friends furnished quite as much aid to the government in proportion to their number, as any other people, both in men and money, and that it was all contributed on the right side.

In 1860 the Friends numbered sixteen congregations with church accommodations for 5280 people. In 1870 the numbers had not sensibly changed. Within a year a new meeting house has been erected in Media, with the capacity of about five hundred seats. With this exception the numbers remain the same, but the church accommodations, it is believed, bear a much larger proportion to the actual members than in other societies.

The earliest form of religious worship by the settlers seems to have been the Lutheran, introduced by the Swedes. Upon the advent of the English this form gave way to that of the church of England, which it much resembles. The first Episcopalians probably associated with the Lutherans in their worship, soon outnumbering and absorbing them. But in 1700 distinct Episcopal organizations began to appear, and the Rev. Mr. Evans was sent from England to attend to their wants. He appears to have officiated for several years after that date at Marcus Hook, Chester, Concord and Radnor.

The first church at Marcus Hook was built in 1702, the first one in Chester in 1704 and the first one in Concord in 1724. The Church of Radnor, now within the limits of Newtown township, was erected in 1717 and is still standing. It is the oldest church building in the county, except that of the Friends in Haverford, which was erected in 1700.

In 1860 the Episcopal congregations numbered seven, with church accommodations for 2325 people. In 1870 the numbers were about the same, and since that date there has been some increase of members, but no changes in congregations or churches.

As a distinct sect the Methodists arose about the period of the American Revolution, and out of that event. For some years prior their had been attempts on the part of John

Wesley and others to awaken, within the Church of England, a livelier interest in practical and devotional christianity. But it is not likely that a new sect would have arisen out of these efforts if the Church of the mother country had not been cut off by the rebellion of the colonies from aiding and controlling its members here. The large majority of the adherents to that form of worship in the colonies, including the more violent Whigs and others of anti-English prejudices, refusing to await the close of hostilities for communication with the mother church, proceeded to organize under the Episcopal form, independent of the Old Country. The minority, embracing the wealthier and more educated portion and also those whose respect for the mother country was greatest, did not unite in this movement. The result was that at the close of the war, there were two Episcopal organizations in the Country, one in accord with the Church of England and the other not.

At that time there was no separate organization in England. But the earnest followers of John Wesley inside the National Church were called Methodists as a term of reproach by their less serious brethern. The name imported here soon ceased to be a term of reproach, and the anti-English Episcopal organization adopted the term of Methodist Episcopal.

Few Methodist churches were built in Delaware County prior to 1800, but since that date this denomination has increased faster than any other. In 1860 the congregations numbered 16, with church accommodations for 4360 people. In 1870 the latter had increased to 7900, and the increase since then has probably been in the same ratio.

Very soon after the first settlement of the English in Pennsylvania, the hardy and enterprising sub-race known as "Scotch-Irish," began to locate among us. These were mainly Presbyterians. They were descendants of the Scotch who had been encouraged to settle in Ireland a few generations before by the British government, and they preserved their national form of religion through the two emigrations.

As it is always the more energetic of any people who leave their homes voluntarily for a new country, each emigration of these Scotchmen took out from the mass the most active, earnest and restless, and this accounts for the peculiar force of character which distinguishes the Scotch-Irish in the new countries. They have really a double distillation of energy.

The first congregation of Presbyterians in this County

met in Middletown at or near the site of the Middletown Presbyterian Church, about a mile west of Media, soon after the beginning of the eighteenth century; certainly before 1735. Others soon followed, but the chief increase of the sect in this County has been since 1820. In 1860 they had seven congregations with church capacity of 2630. In 1870 the former had increased to nine and the latter to 3700. The increase since has been in like proportion.

The first organization of Baptists was in 1715. This was the Brandywine Baptist Church in Birmingham township. Meetings had before that time been held in private houses, and the rite of Baptism was performed in this County as early as 1697. Most of the early Baptists appear to have been previously Friends, and a record bearing date May 4, 1715, quoted by Smith, indicates that these people preserved some of their peculiarities of phraseology after their change.

In 1860 there were five congregations of this denomination in the County, with church accommodations for 2225 people. In 1870 the former had increased to six and the latter to 2500. Since then new churches have been built and new congregations established at South Chester, North Chester, and Media, and the accommodations probably now number 3500. The number of actual members at present is 1463.

The first establishment of Catholics in the county was at the residence of Thomas Willcox, at Ivy Mills, in Concord township, in 1730. The congregation was small and the increase of the sect was very slow until 1835, since then it is quite rapid, mainly from abroad. In 1860 there were five congregations in the county with church accommodations for 1980 people. In 1870 the former had increased to seven and the latter to 2550. The increase since is doubtless at the same rate. In 1757 the number of Catholics in Chester county was 120. Of these probably half resided in the part which is now Delaware county. The number now is not less than 2500.

A beautiful little structure built at Cheyney Station on the West Chester and Philadelphia Railroad, well deserves a notice at this point. It is called the Wayside Church and is independent of all other organizations. It was erected by members of various religious sects, aided by many attached to no denomination, and it is open to all professors of religion, the services being varied to suit the views of the particular officiating individual, who may be some one invited by the congregation, or some well meaning clergyman or other person who may feel it his duty, for the time, to occupy the pulpit. In the absence of such person, services much resembling the Episcopal are read by one of the members designated for the occasion. The congregation numbers about two hundred.

The place owes its origin to the efforts of certain liberal minded people in the neighborhood, whose design appears to be to bring members of the several religious bodies more in contact with one another, that they may learn how insignificant are the differences of opinion which have filled Christendom with persecution and bloodshed. The result is teaching on a small scale the lesson that most religious disputes are purely dialectic. The sects being isolated, learn to attach peculiar and technical meanings to certain much used words, and therefore, to some extent, really talk each a different language from the other without knowing it.

The movement at Cheyney appears to be in the direction of the progress of the age. Within the last half century there is manifestly a growing tendency among the various religious denominations to co-operate with one another in benevolent and humanitarian enterprises, and to view the peculiarities of of one another in a more charitable light; and there is a decreasing disposition on the part of each, to claim the exclusive right of regulating the relations existing between man and his Maker. Delaware County has its full share of the wholesome progress in this direction.

To the history of every county in the Union belongs the subject of slavery and its extinction. In the great struggle all took part on one side or the other. From a very early date our county stood enrolled on the side of human rights. In 1696 the society of Friends, then constituting almost the entire colony, began the contest; first by prohibiting its members from importing slaves, next by proscribing the traffic in them; then by requiring them to be kindly treated and taught to write, and finally one hundred years ago the society abolished slavery among its members.

In 1780 the Legislature of Pennsylvania passed, an act making children born of slave parents after its date free, and requiring those then living to be registered or in default thereof manumitting them. Under this act 146 were registered as slaves for life and sixteen as slaves for a term of years in the part of Chester county which nine years after became Delaware. Of these there were none in the townships of Bethel, Birmingham, Upper Chichester, Upper Providence, Nether Providence and Radnor.

This Act of Assembly was the first instance of the abolition of slavery by legislation in the United States, and it shows that though the government of the State had long before passed out of the hands of the followers of Penn, their hostility to slavery had communicated itself to their fellow-citizens.

The proportion of the descendants of these primitive people is greater in our county than anywhere else in the State, and here too has always been the most universal, quiet, persistent hatred of slavery. This was exhibited in 1850 as well as on other occasions. When the fugitive slave law was passed it provided for the appointment of commissioners in the several counties to carry out its provisions. But in Delaware county no man could be found willing to accept the appointment, and it remained unfilled.

Dr. Smith thinks that the number of slaves in 1776 was not less than three hundred; in 1780 these had doubtless decreased, and though those registered under the act were not all that remained, yet by virtue of the act, those not registered became free, leaving the number after that date 162.

The crusade against the use of intoxicating drinks which began, at least in its extreme violence, about forty years ago, very soon took full possession of this county. Our people by their origin and training were prepared for it. It is curious to contrast 1826 with 1876 in this respect. Then the man who totally abstained from the use of alcohol was supposed by his neighbors to have "a screw loose" somewhere; stands were kept at public sales to supply bidders with what was thought a prime necessity to life, and usually half a dozen fights relieved the monotony of the auctioneer's proceedings. Laborers had their daily allowance of "grog" and children were supposed to run a great risk of life unless provided with their morning dose of "tansy bitters" during the autumn months; visitors knew they were unwelcome unless some intoxicating beverage were offered them; whisky could be had at every corner grocery, at eight or ten cents per quart, as cheap as milk, and many a family dispensed with the useless luxury of a cow that the indispensable substitute might be supplied.

Delaware county was not peculiar in this, nor in the gradual change to a better state of things. But this may be said, that until recently, the improvement here was more thorough and radical than in most other places. We had come to look upon the habitual use of stimulants as a disqualification for any important public or private business.

It is admitted on all sides that the last year or two has presented the aspect of relapse, but the causes are local, and temporary, and the retrograde movement can only be for a time. A community sending so large a proportion of its earnings outside of its borders to purchase that which brought into it only increases the cost of courts, prisons, and almshouses, must soon become poor, and the economy into which it will be forced is upon the road upwards.

The progress of the county in general education has kept pace during the century with its material advancement. One hundred years ago there were no schools in the county for the education of the general public, except a few under the charge of the Society of Friends maintained by private subscriptions. In 1836 the common school system was established, at first as a measure to be accepted or rejected by the townships. Our county at once accepted it, and from that time we have been steadily increasing its efficiency. Now no child however low its circumstances need grow up among us without such training as will develop whatever of intellect he has, and enable him to compete in the race of life on fair terms with the most fortunate.

Beside the public schools, some private institutions deserve notice. Haverford College was established by the Society of Friends in 1833, in Haverford township, on the Pennsylvania Railroad, ten miles from Philadelphia. The farm belonging to the College contains about two hundred acres. The Institution will accommodate about sixty students. The teaching is classical, mathematical and scientific, and is in no sense of the word sectarian.

Swarthmore College, also belonging to the Society of Friends, is upon the West Chester and Philadelphia Railroad, about two miles east of Media. It was founded in 1869. The average number of students is about two hundred and twenty-five, and the whole number of graduates to this time is thirty-five.

This Institution is devoted to the education of both sexes, the projectors being satisfied that under proper care the presence of each will benefit the other, and the result has fully justified the soundness of this view. The course of instruction is the same for both sexes, and the experiment has shown that there is no sensible difference in their capacity for the higher degrees of mental training.

The Crozer Theological Seminary owes its existence to the liberality of the late John P. Crozer and his family. It is located in the Borough of Upland, and it commenced under its present organization in 1868. The endowment of the College is $230,000, and its library has cost $25,000. It is under the charge of the Baptists, and its name denotes its general design. The average number of students is about fifty.

The Pennsylvania Institution for training Feeble Minded Children, established in 1859, near Media, is partly a private charity and partly a public enterprise. The possibility of enabling these unfortunate people to better their condition mentally has only been admitted within the past few years, and the success of this institution renders it no longer a question. Unless in rare cases, in which the intellect is very low indeed, what mind there is has shown itself capable of improvement, in the more fortunate of the class, indeed, until the deficiency becomes scarcely perceptible.

The Delaware County Institute of Science must not be omitted in the history of Delaware County. On September 21st, 1833, five individuals organized this Institution. The number soon increasing, they obtained a charter from the Supreme Court of the State in 1836, and in 1837 built a hall in Upper Providence which was occupied until 1867, when it was abandoned for a new one erected in the Borough of Media. The object of the Association was the promotion of general knowledge, and the establishment of a museum. The founders were George Miller, Minshall Painter, John Miller, Dr. George Smith and John Cassin. Dr. Smith was elected President of the Institute, and he has been annually re-eleeted ever since. He is the only one of the five now living.

The Library of the Institute contains 2000 volumes, and the Museum has become an extensive collection of highly interesting curiosities—Indian Relics, Zoological Specimens, Minerals, Coins, Birds, Insects. The number of members is now 197. The meetings are held monthly, and they furnish matters of interest and utility to those who attend them.

Another subject belonging to the progress of the age requires notice here, because our county is not only in the line of progress in that direction but in the front of the line, and that is the recognition of the rights of humanity independent of the power to enforce them.

Those whom accident or force has made the ruling class are willing at last to carry out to its legitimate consequences the great principle of political ethics that governments derive their just powers only from the consent of the governed.

Hence, men of African descent have been enfranchised. Hence, too, the New Constitution of the State permits women to be elected to offices controlling education; and hence, too, a great political party, a few days ago dared to incorporate among its principles a full recognization of the civil and political rights of women.

We are more worthy to count this advance a part of our county's history for the century, because in our county and in its county town, the first elective office in Pennsylvania ever held by a woman was conferred upon her, and that, too, only a few weeks after it first became possible.

We are entering upon the second century of our national existence. What does it promise us? It will not do to say that there is not just as much room for progress as there was in 1776. The world still moves. To cease developing is to die. It may be said that it is safe to predict so long in advance, for we run small risk of being upbraided with our mistakes. But there is present reason for believing that in 1976 Delaware County will contain a quarter of a million inhabitants, intelligent and industrious, for these are conditions precedent to progress; sober, for intemperance long before that time will either "destroy or be destroyed;" with equal rights in the making and administering of the laws, in the enjoyment of the fruits of the earth, and in the freedom of individual opinions, without distinction on account of sex, race or religion.

www.ingramcontent.com/pod-product-compliance
Lightning Source LLC
LaVergne TN
LVHW011144110826
845150LV00008B/2495

* 9 7 8 1 4 1 8 1 9 1 8 3 2 *